SILVER LININGS

Prayers of
Comfort

A Gift of

new seasons™

Cover illustration: Marian Hirsch

Illustrators: Vivian Browning, Marian Hirsch, Steven Mach

Acknowledgments:

Publications International, Ltd., has made every effort to locate the owners of all copyrighted material to obtain permission to use the selection that appear in this book. Any errors or omissions are unintentional; corrections, if necessary, will be made in future editions.

Scripture quotations marked (NRSV) are taken from the *New Revised Standard Version* of the Bible. Copyright © 1989 by the Division of Christian Education of the National Council of the Churches of Christ in the USA. Used by permission. All rights reserved.

Scripture quotations marked (NIV) are taken from *The Holy Bible, New International Version*®/NIV®. Copyright © 1973, 1978, 1984, International Bible Society. Used by permission of Zondervan Publishing House. All rights reserved.

Scripture quotations marked (TLB) are taken from *The Living Bible.* Copyright © 1971. Used by permission of Tyndale House Publishers, Inc., Wheaton, Illinois 60187. All rights reserved.

Scripture quotations marked (KJV) are taken from *The Holy Bible, King James Version.* Copyright © 1977, 1984, Thomas Nelson Inc., Publishers. All rights reserved.

Scripture quotations marked (NLT) are taken from the *Holy Bible, New Living Translation,* copyright © 1996. Used by permission of Tyndale House Publishers, Inc., Wheaton, Illinois 60187. All rights reserved.

Scripture taken from *The Message,* Copyright © by Eugene H. Peterson, 1993, 1994, 1995. Used by permission of NavPress Publishing Group.

Manufactured in China.

8 7 6 5 4 3 2 1

ISBN: 0-7853-6319-X

Library of Congress Control Number: 2001095713

Contents

Discovering Divine Comfort

*I*n every life, there are times of tragedy. Overwhelmed by grief, we feel lost and alone, unable to regain our footing. Our heart asks, "Will I ever be whole again?"

Desperate to transform our sorrow, we realize we cannot take another step without help from a power greater than ourselves. We must stop trying to control our circumstances and turn our lives over to God. The God who made us is also the God who can heal us.

Suddenly, things become more clear. Hope rises, and something within us stirs back to life; our broken heart senses that healing is afoot. We accept the support of a loving God, whose intent is to move us through our despair so we may grow stronger and more compassionate.

In these life-changing moments, God is at last able to help us. The power of his love is made evident—no other love compares with it. Surely, the most comforting thing during these difficult times is remembering how dear each of us is to God.

Growth takes place in the valleys because God is with us, teaching us and moving us along on our spiritual path. Now, our broken heart rejoices in the knowledge that he was right there with us, sharing our suffering and

encouraging our recovery. The groundwork is prepared, the price of restoration paid. With God's help, we can carry on.

Jesus explains that God loves and looks after us as a shepherd loves and looks after his sheep: "If you had one hundred sheep, and one of them strayed away and was lost in the wilderness, wouldn't you leave the ninety-nine others to go and search for the lost one until you found it? And then you would joyfully carry it home on your shoulders" (Luke 15:4–5 KJV).

So it is with each of us. When we grieve, God's love comes pouring down upon us like sweet, nourishing rain. What was once dry and dead is brought back to life; what was weak is made strong. We test our once-broken wings to find they are whole again, and we take flight.

*God heals the
brokenhearted and binds up
their wounds.*

—Psalm 147:3 NIV

A Healed Heart

Dear God, some of the greatest lessons we learn
are only after our hearts have suffered.
For in times of pain we receive wisdom,
and in times of sorrow we gain understanding.
This is your way of teaching our hearts
that we must know darkness in order to
embrace your light. Thank you for being our
compassionate teacher. Amen.

No matter what deep hurt you
have experienced, He is able to
redeem it. If you allow Jesus to
walk with you . . . He will take
your valley of trouble and give
you a Door of Hope.

—JAN FRANK, *DOOR OF HOPE*

The Window of Opportunity

When the door of one dream slams shut and
we feel trapped by the pain of resignation and
disappointment, we must open our hearts and
our eyes to see the windows just waiting to
fling wide open. We will be led into a whole
new realm of possibility if only we will believe.
Often what God subsequently gives to us is
even more wonderful than that which we lost.

The Lord will guide you
continually, and satisfy your
needs in parched places, and
make your bones strong; you
shall be like a watered garden,
like a spring of water, whose
waters never fail.

—ISAIAH 58:11 NRSV

Creator, I know my life has a purpose, but right now I seem to have lost my way. My head tells me my existence has meaning, but right now my heart cannot discern what it is. I'm sure I am loved, but right now my spirit is too tired to acknowledge it. I ask for direction to find my path again, discernment to understand my purpose, and a grateful heart to see all the blessings that already exist in my life, right now. Amen.

Unbreakable Strength

The resilient heart withstands the winds of change, just as the flexible branch of a tree bends but does not break.

My flesh and my heart may fail,
but God is the strength of my
heart and my portion forever.

—Psalm 73:26 NRSV

When you and I hurt deeply,
what we really need is not an
explanation from God but a
revelation of God. We need to see
how great God is; we need to
recover our lost perspective
on life.

—WARREN W. WIERSBE, *WHY US? WHEN BAD
THINGS HAPPEN TO GOD'S PEOPLE*

*W*eeping may endure for a
night, but joy cometh in the
morning.

—PSALM 30:5 KJV

*God, hear my prayer. Bless me with patience
and a steadfast heart to help me get through
such emotionally trying times. Heal the wounds
of my heart and soul with the soothing balm of
your comforting presence, that I may be able to
love and to live again. Amen.*

*W*hen people disappoint or
hurt me, remind me to look at
you, Lord, instead of them.

—LOIS WALFRID JOHNSON,
YOU'RE MY BEST FRIEND, LORD

Reaching Out in Courage

*It takes great courage to heal, Lord, great
energy to reach out from this darkness to touch
the hem of your garment and ask for healing.
Bless the brave voices telling nightmare tales of
dreadful wounds to the gifted healers of this
world. Together, sufferers and healers are
binding up damaged parts and laying down
burdens carried so long.*

To Begin Again

Dana had considered her marriage to be strong and solid. Jack was a bit controlling and critical of her, but basically they got along well. The thought of divorce had never entered her mind, even during their most vocal fights. So when he came to her one day and told her he was leaving and that he was in love with another woman, she thought the ground had vanished from beneath her.

The day Jack packed up and walked out remained a blur in Dana's mind for months afterward, especially after she discovered Jack had been seeing a mutual good friend of theirs for more than two years. She lost a husband, a friend, and her trust in people in one fell swoop. After a long period of grieving and trying to understand why it had happened, Dana decided the only way she could find peace and move on was to confront Jack and ask him what had gone wrong between them. When she did, Jack treated her coldly, telling her he had never been happy and that they should never have married in the first place. Dana was so anguished that she failed to hear the still, small voice within her telling her Jack was right.

She then began to pray, desperately seeking answers. After a few days, Dana could feel a calming presence watching over her when she prayed, and she heard a clear voice telling her she was and always would be deeply loved.

Dana slowly picked up the pieces of her life. She started with going back to the church she once loved but stopped attending because Jack didn't like it. She took classes she had always wanted to take but never had time for. She called old friends she had drifted away from after she got married. She realized how much of herself she had left behind when she married Jack. She received a clarity that saw beyond the illusion of her "perfect marriage," which, under honest scrutiny, suddenly didn't look that good after all. She knew Jack was right: They never should have married, for they were far too different. What seemed a tragedy became an incredible learning and growing experience for Dana.

Although single life was scary, Dana knew she was never really alone. She had family, good friends, and the love of God on her side. She even let herself be open to one day falling in love again, only this time she would not lose herself in the bargain.

*Lord, I need you here in the midst of
this difficult situation, that the very warmth of
your love will bring about resolution
and that the brightness of your light will
cast out all shadows between us.
Amen.*

From my own tears I have
learned that if you follow your
tears, you will find your heart. If
you find your heart, you will find
what is dear to God. And if you
find what is dear to God, you will
find the answer to how you
should live your life.

—KEN GIRE, *WINDOWS OF THE SOUL*

What a Difference Kindness Makes

Kindness sows a seed within me that begins
to sprout where before all was barren.
Leaves of trust start to bud, and I branch out.
I take in gentle caring and loving nudging and
realize I might just go ahead and bloom!
After all, God arranged spring after winter.

Love makes us greater
than we ever were before,
takes what we have to give
and gives back even more.

Love makes us stronger
than we ever thought we'd be,
takes the load we have to bear
and sets our spirits free.

*W*e all live by hope.
Disappointment occurs when
hopes are not fulfilled, and in
particular when we hope for the
wrong things.... When we live
under the lordship of Christ, our
hopes are surrendered to Him.

—JERRY WHITE,
CHOOSING PLAN A IN A PLAN B WORLD

Silver Linings

*J*ust as each cloud is lined with
silver, so, too, is each painful
experience lined with the miracle
of lessons learned and wisdom
gained. God never takes
something from us without
giving us something else
in return.

*G*od, we know that pain has produced some wisdom in our lives, but it has also created cynicism and fear. People turn on us, reject us, hurt us, and none of us wants to play the fool more than once, so we're tempted to close off our hearts to people and to you. But relationships that bring meaning and joy require vulnerability. Help us trust you to be our truest friend and to lead us to the kind of community that will bring healing rather than destruction.

If your heart has been shattered
    and broken
and your spirit is crippled with
    pain,
you can call on the God of all
    comfort
to bring you to wholeness again.

*God, bless this situation with the gentle,
healing power of your love, that I may find
the courage to carry on through this
dark time of loss and the grace to believe
there is happiness ahead.*
Amen.

*I*f the ground is hard, the rain rolls off. But if the ground is broken, then the rain can soak in and moisten the earth. We've been broken, too . . . so that God can let His healing power flow down through us.

—DOUG WEAD, *A TIME TO LIVE*

Let go and let God see you
    through.
Give in and let God be with you.
Surrender to a love that heals all
    things.
Let go and let God be your
    wings.

God of my heart, I am a broken person.
I do not know how to handle this suffering.
I am not strong enough to do it alone.
Be my strength, God, and do for me
what I simply cannot do for myself.
Be the glue that binds the pieces of my
shattered soul back together, that I may rise
and step back onto the joyful
path of life again.
Amen.

*E*motional wounds may leave no visible physical scars, but deep within, a heart can be suffering. A love gone bad, a relationship that is filled with conflict, shattered friendships, a grudge that will not be settled—they all bring just as much agony as do disasters and physical illnesses.

A special kind of healing is called for when dealing with the wounds of the heart. This must be a healing based on forgiveness, acceptance, and release. To be able to forgive someone who has caused us pain or to let go of a deep resentment requires a maturity and charity that few of us are able to find within ourselves. That is when we need to call upon God, for only God has the power to help us truly forgive and to heal our wounded hearts.

Call to me and I will answer you.

—JEREMIAH 33:3 NRSV

Lift Up Your Heart

Lift up your heart in sweet surrender to the God who is waiting to shower you with blessings. Lift up your soul on wings of joy to the God who is waiting to guide you from the chaos and shadows out into the light of a peace that knows no equal.

When our will is surrendered to God and all its action flows from the power plant of God's will, then disappointment becomes His appointment, and life is no longer a ceaseless struggle to get Him to do something that we think He ought to do.

—ALAN REDPATH, *VICTORIOUS CHRISTIAN LIVING— STUDIES IN THE BOOK OF JOSHUA*

God, I know that you close some doors in my life in order to open new ones. I know that things change and come to an end in order to leave room for new beginnings. Help me have the boldness and enthusiasm to let go of the old and accept the new. Amen.

*H*e will yet fill your mouth with laughter, and your lips with shouts of joy.

—JOB 8:21 NRSV

If I count the things I've asked for that you have not given me, I begin to believe you do not love me, God. But if, instead, I bring to mind all of the goodness you have shown me, I come to trust that you have never given me less than what I need and often have blessed me with far more from a depth of love I cannot comprehend.

*O*ut of sorrow the sweetest souls
have emerged. The most
sympathetic hearts are marked
with scars from wounds which
have healed.

—LEROY BROWNLOW, *JESUS WEPT*

*Lord, help me not accuse you of being untrue
when I don't get from you everything I want,
for you have promised to meet all my needs.
And when I learn to love you supremely and
trust you wholly, my desires will find
fulfillment in you.*

*H*e has sent me to comfort the
brokenhearted.

—Isaiah 61:1 TLB

God, make me an open vessel through which the waters of your Spirit flow freely. Let your love move through me and out into my world, touching everyone I come in contact with. Express your joy through the special talents you have given me, that others may come to know your presence in their own lives by witnessing your presence in mine. Amen.

The Resilient Heart

When someone breaks our heart, we mourn, we grieve, and we feel the pain of rejection. We pray to God for healing and relief. And then we pick up the pieces and, with God's help and guidance, rebuild a heart that is even stronger, more resilient, and ready to love again.

*Dear Lord, thank you for healing my heart
and bringing joy and meaning back into my
life. Thank you for the people who truly care for
me. Help me be a soothing and joyful presence
in their lives as well. Amen.*

Certainly God brings healing, forgiveness, and renewal to all who confess their human failings to him with a repentant heart.

—CHARLES COLSON, *AGAINST THE NIGHT*

Finding Forgiveness

*G*od, when things go wrong, we usually
blame you first. Forgive us for even considering
that you would deliberately hurt one of your
very own children. What could you possibly
have to gain? Thank you for your presence,
and please forgive our many sins.

God's Gentle Power

*T*he God who hung the stars in space will turn
your darkness into light.
The God whose birds rise on the winds will give
your injured soul new flight.
The God who taught the whale its song will
cause your heart to sing again.
For the God whose power made earth and sky
will touch you with his gentle hand.

Lord, far too often we try to
steer the course of our lives
without consulting you, and we
always run into problems. Set us
on a true course that will bring
us closer to you.
Amen.

This is not a choice I would make, for me or for the one who went against my standards, my hopes. It's a riddle, O God, why you give us freedom to choose. It can break our hearts. Comfort me as I cope with a choice not mine; forgive any role I had in it. Help me separate doer from deed as I pass on your words to all: "... nothing can separate us." Not even poor choices I sometimes make myself.

*H*e leads me beside still waters;
he restores my soul.

—Psalm 23:2-3 NRSV

*W*hether my pain is self-
inflicted through sin or stupidity
or imposed by the hurts that
others cause, his grace brings
redemption.

—John F. Westfall, *Enough Is Enough*

*B*ut I call upon God, and the
Lord will save me.

—Psalm 55:16 NRSV

A Risk Worth Taking

The sting of rejection lingers long after it has been inflicted. It often creates an aversion to drawing near to the very thing that can bring healing: love through a relationship with God. It takes a certain willingness to risk reaching out to be forgiven by God if we ever hope to find wholeness again. But there is no more worthwhile risk than that which risks for the sake of God's love.

*W*e need to leave the past with
God. In faith, hope, and trust,
assured of God's forgiveness and
tender understanding, we can
turn away from that which has
brought us so much anguish. We
don't have to carry our regrets
and feelings of guilt with us.

—MILDRED TENGBOM, *GRIEF FOR A SEASON*

Getting Back

*T*hey had been coworkers for 20 years,
close friends for 16 years, business part-
ners for two years, and enemies for 15 months.
What a waste of time. That's what it boiled
down to at this point: a colossal waste of time.

Of course, it was also a waste of money.
Roger cringed just approaching the figures in
his mind. He had never totaled exactly how
much he had lost; he was afraid if he made it
that clear he'd have to hurt Jim, pummel his
face, cause physical harm. The feelings were so

out of character, so unfamiliar, so intensely overwhelming, Roger decided he had better just avoid those feelings.

Roger hated feeling this way. His rage was eating away at him. He found himself snapping at people he loved, being impatient. He was especially frustrated with all the bills. He couldn't get himself to pay them without wanting to throw them across the room. They felt like little reminders of Jim's betrayal, his thieving, tearing down all he had worked so hard to build.

Roger had not understood the depth of Jim's gambling problem, or he would never have entrusted him with so much. He knew Jim liked to bet; heck, he had even accompanied him to the track on weekends. He had not recognized the signs of an addiction out of control, and it was too late now. There was nothing left but debt, Jim's debt, but in reality their joint obligation. Roger had consulted an attorney and discovered that although it was unfortunate, legally, he was liable.

It took a year to untangle the whole mess, but finally he was making headway. He had to go to work for a competitor, a competitor he had been beating. They were happy to have him on their team, but he resented being there.

Roger lost track of Jim. Once the attorneys had finally sorted out who would pay for what and how and when, he had decided to wipe Jim off the face of the earth, at least in his mind. In another year he would finally be free of the financial burden Jim had created. But still it didn't matter; his anger kept building.

Then one day he answered the phone and heard Jim's wife on the line, crying. "I've left Jim," she announced, as if it mattered to Roger. "I'm divorcing him."

Roger didn't know what to say; he felt ill. "There's no one else I can turn to; we have no friends left," she continued. "You were always like an uncle to the kids, please, do you think you can help us?"

"What do you want?" he asked, angry. "I have no money left, you know that."

He was surprised by her answer, "I want my kids to know you, to know that there was a time when their dad was healthy and had friends of your caliber. They need to know that, especially Jimmy."

Roger hung up the phone and went for a walk. He found himself at the deli where he and Jim used to eat lunch. They had shared their dreams, their hopes, their worries, as they outlined their plan to start their own business. It had been brilliant; it really had. It would have been very successful. Tears stung Roger's eyes. He walked on. He found himself praying, nothing formal, just talking inside his head.

He walked by the junior high school. He stood there thinking about his son and Jim's son. His own son was going to be OK. The past year and a half had been very hard on his family, but it was getting better. He felt his anger coalescing, transforming from liquid to solid, like the gelatin candy his daughter liked to eat.

A couple of years ago he had taken a Bible study course at church on forgiveness. He thought it would be naive, a class on turning the other cheek. The nun had surprised him.

"Enabling evil, ignoring sin, is not forgiveness," she had explained. "Sometimes simply healing the hurt in you they have caused is forgiveness enough; you are releasing them from the consequences of their actions, and that is a great gift." Yes, that was forgiveness. He was clearing up the debt Jim created and wounded him with; perhaps that was forgiveness enough.

Roger found himself back at his home, hand on the phone.

"Hello?" Jim's wife's voice on the other end of the line startled him, even though he had placed the call. He heard a voice, his own voice, saying, "I'm calling you back because I've been thinking. Why don't I pick Jimmy up on Saturday, and I'll take the boys to lunch and to see a game. Tell Jimmy I'll be there at 11:30. Tell Jimmy I'll be there."

He had found another way of forgiving, even of loving his enemy; he would help heal the children.

… there is a depression among
true Christians, with the
individuals who are out of
the center of God's directive will.
The most unhappy person in
the world is a child of God
out of the Father's control.
The cure is to return!

—F. L. WHITESELL, *THE CURE FOR DEPRESSION*

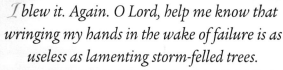

*I blew it. Again. O Lord, help me know that
wringing my hands in the wake of failure is as
useless as lamenting storm-felled trees.
Give me eyes to see beyond chaos to possibilities.
In that way, I won't miss finding out what
could happen if I picked up a saw and took to
that tree, making firewood around which
friends can gather.*

Moving Past Resentment

*Forgiveness is not easy. Often it requires us to
become far more than we were before;
more mature, more accepting, and more
compassionate. But once we forgive and
stretch ourselves, we can never go back to
being that unforgiving and resentful person we
were before. We have been opened up,
expanded, and set free.*

*Dear God, the wound between this person
and me seems too deep to heal, and the chasm of
misunderstanding seems too wide to leap across.
I pray for guidance that I may do my part
to close the wound and narrow the gap
between us with love, understanding
and forgiveness.
Amen.*

*A*s the one perfect, loving Father, He welcomes our coming to Him—even spilling out our tears, our sorrow, or our heartache. Bring it all into His presence. He not only will accept your heart cry, He will comfort you.

—JACK HAYFORD, *I'LL HOLD YOU IN HEAVEN*

*B*e kind to one another, tenderhearted, forgiving one another, as God in Christ has forgiven you.

—EPHESIANS 4:32 NRSV

*U*nforgiveness is an acid which
does more damage to the vessel
in which it is stored than the
victim on which it is poured.
I had to face the fact that my
emotional and spiritual, as well
as physical, healing waited on my
determination to forgive.

—Barbara Taylor, *From Rejection to
Acceptance*

*God, I pray for the strength and the wisdom
to know what to do in this situation.
I pray for enough love to forgive this person for
the pain they have caused me and to forgive
myself for the ill will I have harbored against
this person. Help me be a truly forgiving
person so that the weight of resentment may
be lifted from my shoulders.
Amen.*

The Gift of Forgiveness

*The greatest gift we can offer someone is our
forgiveness, for it has the dual power to set the
other person free and to set us free as well.*

*I've been driven many times to
my knees by the overwhelming
conviction that I had nowhere
else to go.*

—ABRAHAM LINCOLN

Signs of Possibility

*From my dark corner I look up and see
wings fluttering against the window and know
that a God who can make a butterfly
from a caterpillar can surely make
something new of me.*

*T*hen you will know the truth,
and the truth will set you free.

—JOHN 8:32 NIV

*H*is is a loving, tender hand, full
of sympathy and compassion.

—DWIGHT L. MOODY,
ANECDOTES AND ILLUSTRATIONS

*Pain can be a signal,
a reminder to reach out to
God for help. Let us always
act on that signal.*

Escape
From Pain

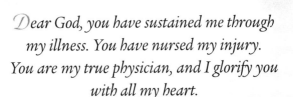

Dear God, you have sustained me through my illness. You have nursed my injury. You are my true physician, and I glorify you with all my heart.
Amen.

The Problem With Pain

Pain in its countless forms can test us to our limits; it can seem to overwhelm us at times and plunge us into discouragement and even despair. Is it possible for us to handle such debilitating pain? The kind that's always there, every morning and every night—pain that's relentless?

The answer is that it *is* possible. When it hurts too much to even pray, when pain overwhelms us, God is present—close and caring—even before we are able to ask. God can and will get us through. He provides friends to encourage us and pray for us, doctors and medicine to heal us, and the faith and strength we need to conquer whatever pain we face.

When All Is Not Well

*When illness strikes, the effects go beyond the
physical suffering. Fear, despair, and terrible
isolation arise as the illness prolongs itself.
It feels natural to lash out at your failing body,
medicine that does not help, and even at the
God who allowed this terrible thing to
happen to you. The fate of the patient's loved
ones can be equally painful, as they stand by
feeling helpless to be of any real assistance. Yet,
be assured that the Lord is there among you.*

*R*ejoice in hope, be patient in
suffering, persevere in prayer.

—ROMANS 12:12 NRSV

Dance

Your soul can dance though pain
   is here.
Call healing music to your ear.
Spot emotion's fickle turning,
Leap in love,
Stretch hopes,
Master fear's deep strains.
Dare to dance both health and
   pain.
However clumsy, long, or
   fleeting,
We dance life well if grace is
   leading.

*Despite today's valley of shadow and sickness,
I know you, shepherd of my soul, will continue
restoring me as I move through treatment to the
safe meadow of wellness.*

*Is illness your will, Lord? I need answers,
for I want you to help me heal. But if you send
illness, how can I trust you to heal? Reassure
me that you will work everything out
eventually. And when that isn't possible,
be with me as I suffer. Freed from fear I can get
stronger as your healing energy flows through
me, restoring me to my abundant life.*

Splinter

*Such a tiny sliver of wood to cause such sharp
pain. Yet it reminds me to pray for those with
far more serious hurts.*

*Help me recover from this ambush of illness,
Great Physician, and the worry it brings.
Reassure my fearful heart that my sickness was
never intended; it just happened. Bodies break
down, parts age, and minds weary. Your
assurance gives me strength to hang on.*

Job was in great pain, yet he
could say of God, "Though he
slay me, yet will I trust in him."

—JOB 13:15 KJV

God whispers to us in our
pleasures, speaks in our
conscience, but shouts in our
pains: it is His megaphone to
rouse a deaf world.

—C. S. LEWIS, *THE PROBLEM OF PAIN*

The Faith to Climb Mountains

*If we have but faith the size of a mustard seed,
we can ascend this mountain of suffering and
descend into the valley of serenity, which is on
the other side.*

*The final healing, O God, is near, and my body
is painfully ready. Help me think of this as a
"birthing pain," for I'm in the process of
becoming new. Deliver me onto that other shore
newly born and healed from this life's travail.
Hold my hand, for pain's waves are
building into a sea strong enough for us
to walk across at last.*

I can rely on Him alone—for
physical strength as for every
other need.

—CATHERINE MARSHALL, *A CLOSER WALK*

*Thank you, Great Physician, for this chance—
this second chance at life. Forgive me for being
surprised, as if healing were beyond possibility
and your intention.*

Thankful

*Thank God when the pain ends, when once
again we're well and whole and strong.
Thank God when our bodies are released from
the blinding, mind-numbing hurts that affect
our whole lives. Thank God when we have
complete victory over pain.*

Sometimes pain can burn so deep, scorching away at the center of self, bringing utter darkness and despair—yet even in this most terrible pain, we can turn to you, Lord, for courage, comfort, strength, and the victory you so lovingly offer us, giving us light and hope to see us through.

Jesus said, "Very truly, I tell you,
you will weep and mourn...you
will have pain, but your pain will
turn into joy."

—JOHN 16:20 NRSV

Guiding Light

*In the midst of the darkness that threatens to
overwhelm us lies a pinpoint of light,
a persistent flicker that guides us through the
pain and fear, through the hopelessness and
despair, to a place of peace and healing
on the other side. This is God's Spirit,
leading us back home like the lighthouse
beacon that directs the ships through the fog
to the safety of the harbor.*

Testing, Testing

*Scared as much of the tests as of their findings,
I shiver while flimsily gowned and alone on
this side of a diagnosis. Closing my eyes and
breathing deeply, I feel God's warming presence
around my shoulders.*

*Lord, help them, comfort them, and bring
them peace and sweet, pain-free sleep.
Ease the tension in their bodies and the ache
in their hearts. Heal their hurts, please, Lord,
and let them rest easy.*

O, I have suffered
With those that I saw suffer.

—WILLIAM SHAKESPEARE, *THE TEMPEST*

Our Deliverer

*Praise the Lord, for he has seen the affliction
and heard the groans of his people—both his
children who were slaves in Egypt and us who
were in bondage to physical pain. Indeed, he has
come to me in my darkest moment and rescued
me from my misery. He is a compassionate and
wonderful God, who loves his children and
watches over each one of us.*

Can't Breathe!

Waking in the lonely darkness of night,
I gasped for air, fighting to breathe,
feeling pain sear through my aching lungs. Fear
clutched me. What if my lungs tightened so
much that I couldn't breathe at all? What if I
couldn't even draw breath to call for help?
What if nobody came to help me, and I died
there alone in the night?

The fear wasn't new to me. Not being able
to breathe brings a special terror many people

don't understand. For most people, breathing isn't even something they think about. It's taken for granted, as normal as walking, talking, and eating. For me, breathing was a gift to be treasured and appreciated because there were terrible times when every breath came as a struggle.

The pain might strike me for almost no apparent reason. A puff of dust in my face. A whiff of dry laundry detergent. An especially cold day with air so frigid that it tightens my lungs. Even powdered drink mix might cause my lungs to tighten and my breathing to rasp.

The worst, though, were those horrible nights when I'd abruptly jolt awake, unable to catch my breath, feeling that ominous tension in my chest. Who knew why asthma struck while I slept, but it often did, and I was never entirely braced for it. I knew that fear and tension would only make it worse, but not being able to breathe always caught me off guard and terrified me.

I grew up with asthma, with emergency visits to the doctor, with shots, and with small purple pills tucked under my tongue.

I missed more school than anyone I knew, spending many days propped up against pillows while I worked at sucking in enough air to keep from blacking out. By the time an attack ended, my arm and back muscles throbbed as if I'd worked out for hours.

I finally outgrew the asthma, and I thought I was done with it. Years later, however, it struck again, only more suddenly and harder somehow. My family and I were forced to adjust, searching for medications to control the attacks and ease my breathing. There were shots and inhalers of various kinds, visits to the doctor, and experimenting to find the right medication for me.

Then there were the sudden, sharp attacks and times when the inhalers meant to open my lungs seemed to do just the opposite. There were times when the shots worked far too slowly or when the medications caused other serious side effects. Meanwhile, I struggled, full of fear and distress, not knowing if I'd even survive this frightening disease. Asthma doesn't have a cure, and many still die from it.

Alone in the darkest part of the night, not wanting to disturb my family every time I woke with my lungs tightening and fear wrenching my mind, I battled not just the disease but also the fear of that disease. Often, I wasn't sure I'd win. Often, I felt weak and helpless and desperate.

In those fearful struggles, each time an attack gripped me, I would silently cry out to God for his help, his comfort, and his soothing calm to ease my fears. He was always there, each time I sought him. I felt his presence as my breathing calmed and steadied again.

He got me through many long, sleepless, fear-filled nights until we found a balance of medications to keep my breathing steady and my lungs open. Through those lonely, painful, frightening nights, God always heard my wordless, breathless cries, and he always helped me triumph over the pain and the fear of not being able to breathe.

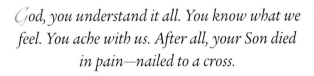

God, you understand it all. You know what we feel. You ache with us. After all, your Son died in pain—nailed to a cross.

What I Do Know

I don't know which is worse, the wrenching physical pain or the emotional anguish with it. What I do know is that he will take care of all my hurts.

So we do not lose heart. Even though our outer nature is wasting away, our inner nature is being renewed day by day.

—2 CORINTHIANS 4:16 NRSV

Moody Blues

Illness makes our moods like a children's wind-up toy, crazily up one minute, flat down the next; we cry and laugh, we worry and celebrate! Getting well is hard, complicated work. May God lead us into full recovery, but carefully—we're still a bit unpredictable.

My Creator, blessed is your presence. For you and you alone give me power to walk through dark valleys into the light again. You and you alone give me hope when there seems no end to my suffering. You and you alone give me peace when the noise of my life overwhelms me. I ask that you give this same power, hope, and peace to all who know discouragement, that they, too, may be emboldened and renewed by your everlasting love.
Amen.

Piercing Pain

How can you explain excruciating pain to
someone who's never had it? The jolt of pain—it
hurts to move, to think, to hear, to be.
And what thankfulness when it's gone!

Somebody Knows

Nobody knows someone else's pain, how much
she or he hurts, the depth and power of it.
Nobody can know for sure. Nobody
knows . . . except the Lord.

The Best Medicine

*The best medicine for a discouraged spirit is a
dose of love. Add a touch of support from
friends and family, mix with a pinch of
awareness of God's presence, and spread over
your entire heart and soul. Wait ten seconds,
then smile. Nothing can withstand such a
powerful healing balm.*

*Of the many ways to suffer, I feel all of them in
this firestorm of sadness. It robs my sleep,
saps my strength, and changes me so much I
hardly recognize myself. Ease my misery, Lord.
Clear my mind as though washing streaks
from a window. Hold me when I cry,
releasing feelings that keep me sick;
send others to hold me, too. Remind me that
this pain is temporary and can be relieved,
just like my worries.*

These troubles and sufferings of ours are, after all, quite small and won't last very long. Yet this short time of distress will result in God's richest blessing upon us forever and ever! So we do not look at what we can see right now, the troubles all around us, but we look forward to the joys in heaven which we have not yet seen. The troubles will soon be over, but the joys to come will last forever.

—2 Corinthians 4:17–18 TLB

Lord, I am now in tribulation,
and my heart is ill at ease, for I
am much troubled with the
present suffering.... Grant me
patience, O Lord, even now in
this moment. Help me, my God,
and then I will not fear, how
grievously soever I be afflicted.

—THOMAS Á KEMPIS, *THE IMITATION OF CHRIST*

Refilling the Emptiness

*Illness has come like a thief in the night and
stolen the innocence of daily, take-it-for-granted
life. In God's hands, it can become an
opportunity for renewal and discovering
what—and who—really matters.*

*Sitting here in this waiting room, O God,
time drags and fear festers. Remake worry into
energized, active prayers, into trust in the
process of healing and recovery. We're scooting
over to make room for you, a companion
for the waiting.*

Spare Me?

*I'd like to pray to be spared of all pain, but life
is full of pain. No one escapes it. Better to ask
God to be near whenever it comes.*

In the Hospital

*So much pain and misery all in one place.
No wonder so many people avoid hospitals.
Yet there are nurses, doctors, aids, volunteers,
all those health workers who have committed
their lives to ending pain and who are
there for us all.*

*Why is there so much pain in the world, God?
It's so hard to understand. Lord, help us
through it all. Help us comprehend or at least
simply trust in you.*

Then the Lord said [to Moses],
"I have observed the misery of
my people who are in Egypt; I
have heard their cry on account
of their taskmasters. Indeed, I
know their sufferings, and I have
come down to deliver them from
the Egyptians, and to bring them
up out of that land to a good
and broad land, a land flowing
with milk and honey."

—Exodus 3:7–8 NRSV

Dear God, the pain is so great and unbearable that I feel as though another moment of it will tear me apart. Please rescue me from this pain. Touch my body and heal me. Hear my pleas for only you have the power to deliver me from my affliction. Have mercy upon me. I cry out to you day and night, and I will turn to no one but you.

Look upon mine affliction and
my pain.

—PSALM 25:18 KJV

Dear Lord, each night the news is full of
trouble. So much pain and sorrow. It makes me
ache to see it all. Some nights, it seems that's all
there is; this world seems sometimes so weary
and heavy laden. Then I turn to you and know
that you are nearest on the darkest days.
And there is comfort in knowing you and that
you have not forsaken us or the people whose
world is presently dark.
Amen.

Watch Care

When Polly can't feed herself, Sam bends to
help her. When she falters in mid-step, lost in her
own mind, he guides her steps. When she weeps
in confusion, in pain, or in fear, he comforts her
and in caring for her finds easing of his own
pain. In sickness and in health, Sam had vowed,
and now he keeps his promise.

The call of God involves earthly suffering because through it we may magnify His power to keep us and demonstrate His grace in our weakness. Earthly suffering, bravely borne, shows powerfully the reality of the living God.

—STUART BRISCOE, *WHEN THE GOING GETS TOUGH*

Out of Pain

The story went that he was in pain, constant pain, and from the center of all that hurt, they say he created wonderful music, bringing something truly good out of it.

But in the meantime, God is
able to use our suffering to
glorify Himself. It is not wasted!

—Joni Eareckson Tada, *Glorious Intruder*

*Lord, when it hurts too much to even pray,
when pain overwhelms us, you are still here,
close and caring.*

*Call on me in the day of
trouble; I will deliver you, and
you shall glorify me.*

—Psalm 50:15 NRSV

Never-Ending Peace

Do you get anxious at sunrise because all you can see is the tiny rim of the sun? No, because you know that if you wait long enough, you will see the sun in all its brilliance. The same is true of God's plan for your life. You will never see everything in advance, but if you wait long enough, God always reveals his will.

Relax, God Is in Charge

We become discouraged when we try to live according to our own time clocks.
We want what we want, and we want it this very minute. Then, when we don't get it, we sink in the quicksand of hopelessness and defeat. Only when we realize that God is at work in our lives will we begin to relax and let things happen in due season. Fruit will not ripen any faster because we demand it but will ripen in all its sweet splendor when it is ready in spite of our demands.

*G*ive your life with all its stress
to Him and say, "Lord, please
give me a new life. Replace the
pressure I feel with the peace You
offer. Help me follow Your
principles of stress
management."

—RICHARD WARREN, *ANSWERS TO LIFE'S
DIFFICULT QUESTIONS*

Lord, the clamor of my life is unbearable. People pressing in on all sides. Decisions crying out to be made. Problems needing to be solved. I don't want to get out of bed in the morning. I want to hide, to escape. Please help me!

Only a Prayer Away

When we place ourselves into the care of a loving God, things that we once thought impossible now brim with possibility. That which had eluded us seems right within our grasp, and we rest in the knowledge

that all the guidance and support we need is never more than a prayer away.

Lord, give me hope,
Give me patience to cope
And a reason to keep on trying.
Take my trembling hand
Give me power to stand
And a faith that is strong and
   undying.

—BARBARA ROBERTS PINE, "LORD, GIVE ME HOPE"

*D*on't fret or worry. Instead of worrying, pray. Let petitions and praises shape your worries into prayers, letting God know your concerns. Before you know it, a sense of God's wholeness, everything coming together for good, will come and settle you down. It's wonderful what happens when Christ displaces worry at the center of your life.

—PHILIPPIANS 4:6–7 *THE MESSAGE*

Amazing Grace

*God's grace is our comfort in times of trouble
and our beacon of hope amid the blackness
of despair. By opening ourselves to God's
ever-present grace, we know we are loved
and cared for, and our hearts sing out
in joyful gratitude.*

Do not let your hearts be
troubled. Believe in God, believe
also in me. . . . Peace I leave with
you; my peace I give to you.
I do not give to you as the world
gives. Do not let your hearts be
troubled, and do not let them
be afraid.

—JOHN 14:1, 27 NRSV

Pieces of a Dream

*How often we mourn a shattered dream,
a goal not met, a vision unfulfilled. Yet amid the
pieces of one shattered dream often lie the
makings of an even grander design for our life.
What sometimes appears as a disappointing
ending is, in truth, the beginning of a whole new
and exciting road ahead.*

When Frustration Comes to Call

*W*hen we talk about frustration, we generally mean those feelings brought about by shocking changes in our worldly circumstances. Loss of loved ones, loss of property, loss of a job, disappointed expectations. These events, and so many others, leave us feeling frustrated and helpless. "How could this happen to me?" we ask. "Who did this to me?"

The hard lesson is that even though the events that led to our frustration seemingly came out of nowhere, the solution will not. It's up to us to quit trying to figure out how this happened and turn our attention to what we can do about it. Frustration leaves us feeling out of control, prey to random forces. When frustrated, we must learn to seek out the areas we can control and learn to accept that the ultimate controller of our circumstances is always watching out for us.

*L*et us therefore approach the
throne of grace with boldness,
so that we may receive mercy
and find grace to help in
time of need.

—HEBREWS 4:16 NRSV

In Due Season

Stop moaning and asking,
    "Why, God, why?"
There is always a meaningful
    reason.
Stop whining and pleading,
    "When, God, when?"
For good things will arrive in
    due season.
We are promised that God's
    never early,
But neither is God ever late.
All the blessings we wish will
    come to us
When we learn to have faith
    while we wait.
When I am lost and discouraged,
And there seems to be no hope
    in sight,
I turn my cares over to the God
    of my heart,
And his love lets my spirit take
    flight.

*D*on't worry about anything;
instead, pray about everything;
tell God your needs and don't
forget to thank him for the
answers. If you do this you will
experience God's peace, which is
far more wonderful than the
human mind can understand.
His peace will keep your
thoughts and your hearts quiet
and at rest as you trust in
Christ Jesus.

—PHILIPPIANS 4:6-7 TLB

*J*esus said to his followers, "I tell
you, do not worry about your
life, what you will eat, or about
your body, what you will wear.
For life is more than food and
the body more than clothing."

—LUKE 12:22-23 NRSV

Our Provider

*One of the Hebrew names for God is Jehovah
Jireh (JY-rah). Besides having a nice ring to it,
its meaning—"God, our provider"—is one
worth remembering. In life, we may experience
times of abundance and also times when we
struggle to make ends meet. In any situation,
God asks us to trust and honor him
as Jehovah Jireh, the God who provides
all that we truly need.*

Oh Lord, I do not know how to deal with this person. I am afraid and angry, and my heart aches with sadness. I turn to you, God, and ask for the peace that passes all understanding. I surrender the yoke of my burden to you, that your will be done, not mine. Let me rest in the healing waters of your ever-present Spirit, now and forever. Amen.

Breaking the Chains of Discouragement

When someone we love is trapped in a prison of defeat and discouragement, we can help them break free of the chains that bind them by doing these three things: supporting their deepest dreams, believing in their gifts and talents, and loving and accepting them for who they are at this very moment.

*God, when life feels like a ride that won't
let us off, remind us that you are waiting for us
to reach up to you. And when we finally do,
thank you for being there to lift us to
peace and safety.*

The Provision

Cameron had lost his job due to company downsizing. Because he was always industrious and reliable, Cameron was taken off guard when the pink slip landed on his desk. "I'd never been fired in my life," he said dejectedly. Moreover, since many companies were laying off employees in Cameron's area of expertise, it was not a good time to be looking for a job.

As the sole provider for his wife and two growing sons, Cameron didn't have long to be out of work before the family's savings would be depleted. The unemployment checks were not nearly enough to meet the monthly budget, but days and then weeks came and went until several months had passed, and Cameron could not secure even an interview in his specialized field of experience and training.

"The stress was tremendous, and it was having a very negative effect on our family life," Cameron confessed. "I began to have an urgent sense that if I didn't change my perspective and attitude, we weren't going to make it through."

Cameron and his wife spent long hours talking about what they needed to do to hold things together. Finally, based on what they knew about God's promises and their situation, they decided they had to make a sincere effort to stop worrying about what would happen and, instead, start praying and taking God at his word.

Together Cameron and his wife made a list of their debts and bills and the amount they needed to meet each, and together they spent time each day asking God to guide Cameron's search for work and to provide for the family's needs. "When we put our energies into whatever God gave us to do and didn't sweat what the future would bring, an amazing calm came over our household," Cameron said. "Odd jobs kept opening up for me to do. And I always had just enough work to meet the financial obligations we had."

As an act of gratitude and trust in God's promise to provide for his family's needs, Cameron gave a certain percentage of his income to a nonprofit organization that reached out to needy people in the community. "I couldn't help but give. God was so faithful to us. During the entire time I was out of work, our car never broke down, my children's clothes and shoes did not wear out, we had no unexpected or emergency expenses, and there was always just enough money to pay the bills and put food on the table. God took care of us in every way."

Cameron's "odd jobs" evolved into a home business that specializes in estimating damages and doing cleanup for small businesses that experience floods, fires, and other similar disasters. As a team, Cameron and his wife take care of all aspects of the company, and they have enjoyed moderate success in their business.

"I'm not rich," Cameron smiles, "but it's a living, and we're still here."

As far as Cameron is concerned, that year of nip-and-tuck living was a seminar in learning to let go of the illusion of being in control of his own life and finding what it really means to trust God's provision. "When you have a family counting on you to feed them, to give them a house to live in, and to buy the clothes they need, it becomes a heavy load when you lose the means to do that. But that's the very thing that brought me face to face with the reality that I need God's help to be able to meet the responsibilities he has given me."

"It's not an experience I'd care to repeat," Cameron chuckled, "but it's not one I would trade for a million dollars. It may sound clichéd, but money cannot buy the personal growth nor the insights that I gained during that struggle. And the best part is that God has become so much more real to me. Seeing his intervention in my life made me know that God's love is not just theoretical or for everyone else. Now I believe beyond a shadow of a doubt that he cares about me, too."

Below the Surface

*It's easy to become tired and discouraged when
we can see little or no progress being made
toward our goals and dreams. Often, it looks as
if nothing is happening, and we become
frustrated and want to give up. But we must
remember that although the surface of a pond
often appears still and quiet, there is ever-
abundant activity of life going on just below.*

He gives power to the faint and
strengthens the powerless.

—Isaiah 40:29 NRSV

Those who love me, I will
deliver; I will protect those who
know my name. When they call
to me, I will answer them; I will
be with them in trouble, I will
rescue them and honor them.

—Psalm 91:14–15 NRSV

*Dear Lord, my financial demands exceed the
resources I have. The pressure I feel to do
something, even if it's unwise, is building,
and I fear I will cave in and make a decision
I will regret. Help me trust you. Preserve
my integrity and show me your way of
dealing with this situation.*

My brothers and sisters,
whenever you face trials of any
kind, consider it nothing but joy,
because you know that the
testing of your faith produces
endurance; and let endurance
have its full effect, so that you
may be mature and complete,
lacking in nothing.

—JAMES 1:2-4 NRSV

Time to Go Home?

Money rolled in and the living
was fine:
God was in his place, and I safe
in mine.
But something went wrong; now
bills stand in piles.
I guessed I'd call God from
"across the miles."
I expected he'd moved, but he
was still there—
Said I could return and find rest
in his care.
"But money!" I cried. "That's my
problem now;
I've got to pay bills, and I don't
quite know how."
On the heels of my lament came
his quiet reply:
"Dear child, just come home; at
the right time, I'll supply."

Lord, we don't like to let stress destroy our even keel, but sometimes it does. We need your wisdom to help us manage the load and your grace to keep us from being ill-tempered.

Trust in the Lord with all your
heart and lean not on your own
understanding;
in all your ways acknowledge
him, and he will make your
paths straight.

—PROVERBS 3:5-6 NIV

Beyond Discouragement

Discouragement comes in many forms; no matter what the source, it exhausts the spirit and drains the soul. Without help, we feel as though we are drowning in a smothering well of darkness. Without hope, we want to give up. We want to give in. We want to wave the white flag of defeat.

When the obstacles that arise in our path seem insurmountable, and the challenges we face appear beyond our capability, that is when we most need to turn our lives over to a power greater than ourselves. Indeed, there is tremendous healing power in that moment of surrender when our discouraged spirit feels it has reached its limit, for this is the moment when we are able to let go and let God take over.

*T*hose of steadfast mind you
keep in peace—in peace because
they trust in you.

—Isaiah 26:3 NRSV

The Power of Creativity

*The creative power within is your power to
overcome any obstacle and break through any
binding walls that keep you from your dreams.
This power was given to you by the greatest of
all creators, the One who created you, God. Just
look around at the amazing beauty and
diversity of the world you live in, and you will
never again doubt that God supports your
creative endeavors.*

Jesus said, "Come to me, all you
that are weary and are carrying
heavy burdens, and I will give
you rest."

—MATTHEW 11:28 NRSV

Like the Water Lily

*We can take a lesson from the precious
water lily. For no matter what outside force or
pressure is put upon the lily, it always rises
back to the water's surface again to feel the
nurturing sunlight upon its leaves and petals.
We must be like the lily, steadfast and true
in the face of every difficulty, that we too may
rise above our problems and feel God's light
upon our faces again.*

Those who hope in the Lord will
renew their strength. They will
soar on wings like eagles; they
will run and not grow weary,
they will walk and not be faint.

—Isaiah 40:31 NIV

Thank you, Lord, for helping us through our hard times. You have shown your love for us and made us more compassionate people. Help us show the same love to others who are going through hard times.

The Beginning of Faith

All too often it is not until we reach our rope's end that we find an opportunity for the beginning of faith.

Cast all your anxiety on him,
because he cares for you.

—1 PETER 5:7 NRSV

*Through the darkest days,
God walks beside me and will
never leave me. His presence
comforts me and gives me the
courage to keep going no
matter what the
circumstances are.*

*From the Ashes
Comes Hope*

*Why tornadoes, Lord? Why typhoons or fires?
Why floods or earthquakes? Why devastating
accidents or acts of terror, Lord? It's so hard to
understand. Perhaps there is no way to find any
sense in overwhelming circumstances. Perhaps
it's about trusting in you, God, no matter
what comes and leaving it in your hands,
where it belongs because, in fact, you do really
love us and care about us and will make
things work out for us.*

When the earth and all its
people quake, it is I who hold its
pillars firm.

—Psalm 75:3 NIV

Filling the Empty Spaces

When violence strikes us like mud splashed from a puddle, we bolt our doors and cover our heads. God can draw us from hiding and nudge us to get busy. For violence, like water in a puddle, can only thrive in a hole. Inspired, we can fill it up with hands that, instead of wringing helplessly, are busy rebuilding.

*Y*ou cannot control every
circumstance, but you can
respond to each one in faith.

—ELLIS MORRISON, *LIFE HURTS—GOD HEALS!*

*S*ave me, O God,
for the floodwaters are up to my neck.
Deeper and deeper I sink into the mire;
I can't find a foothold to stand on.
I am in deep water,
and the floods overwhelm me.
I am exhausted from crying for help;
my throat is parched and dry.
My eyes are swollen with weeping,
waiting for my God to help me...
Answer my prayers, O Lord,
for your unfailing love is wonderful.

—PSALM 69:1–3, 16 NLT

By Candlelight

While terror rages, we cling together by candlelight, drawing courage from one another until the dawn comes again. It is then that God will bring us a happier day.

You who have made me see many troubles and calamities will revive me again; from the depths of the earth you will bring me up again. You will increase my honor, and comfort me once again.

—PSALM 71:20–21 NRSV

He's Always There for Us

Disaster can strike at any time without warning to anyone anywhere. Our lives can change dramatically in one unexpected moment, but in the worst times of our lives, we can lean on family, friends, and even strangers who reach out to us. Yet, even more importantly, we can turn to God, who is always there for us during our darkest hours. He will never fail us, never let us down, and never turn away from us when we cry out to him.

All around, the storms may
   churn,
the seas may rage, the fires burn.
But deep within, you will not
   fear,
you will have peace when
   centered there.
For even amidst the tempest
   wild,
God will be there to guide you,
   child.

—BARBARA ROBERTS PINE, "ALL AROUND,
   THE STORMS MAY CHURN"

Why, O God, do bad things happen?
Can I be angry when I pray?
It's all I have to offer.
I find relief sharing it with you;
for now, that's all I need.

Certain Comfort

*We have seen that unconceivable acts
can cause our world to crumble around us.
Yet we need not fall apart inside. If we place our
trust in God's goodness, he will come to our aid
and bring us comfort to restore our hope in the
future. His love and compassion will lift our
spirits so we can rejoice no matter what disaster
or tragedy may befall us. For as long as God is
beside us, nothing can defeat us or take what is
truly important from us.*

If the Lord had not been my
help, my soul would soon have
lived in the land of silence.

—Psalm 94:17 NRSV

Choosing Hope

Like a speed bump in a parking lot, a decision lies in our path, placed there by God to remind us hope is a choice. Choosing to live as people of hope is not to diminish or belittle pain and suffering or lie about evil's reality. Rather it is to cling to God's promise that he will make all things new.

*S*urely there is a future, and your
hope will not be cut off.

—PROVERBS 23:18 NRSV

The raging storm may round
   us beat,
A shelter in the time of storm;
We'll never leave our safe retreat,
A shelter in the time of storm.
Oh, Jesus is a Rock in a weary
   land,
A weary land, a weary land;
Oh, Jesus is a rock in a weary
   land,
A shelter in the time of storm.

—VERNON J. CHARLESWORTH,
"A SHELTER IN THE TIME OF STORM"

From a Tiny Seed, Bloom

*With God's hand tending it, even the tiniest
seed of hope cannot be dislodged.*

*Oh Lord, when I see terrible, fearful events—
explosions destroying whole buildings, droughts
that turn crops to dust, storms devastating all in
their path—then I turn to you. And you are
always here, listening, caring, and waiting for
all of us to reach out to you.*
Amen.

Curled Up in a Closet

The wind hurled rain against my sliding glass door, and I thought it might smash the glass at any moment. Meanwhile, I watched the dark clouds race across the sky. As the surrounding trees shook violently, I worried that they'd snap off and fly against my trembling windows. When I stepped outside, I heard police officers with their bullhorns call out warnings from their patrol cars.

I'd been glued to my portable radio once the power failed across the city. According to the broadcaster, the entire midsection of the country was under siege. Storm after storm tore across 13 states, producing terrible tornadoes, more than ever before in such a brief time. Word had gradually filtered through, telling of entire communities destroyed, towns leveled, property severely damaged, and lives lost. Reports were still sketchy. With power down and storm damage extensive, news came slowly, and rumors spread quickly. It was hard to believe such frightening things were occurring all around us.

I'd never been in a tornado nor seen anything like this before. Fear gripped my heart, and I kept silent beside the radio, listening for news and praying that none of the series of powerful tornadoes would suddenly plow through our city. Through that endless, sleepless night, I fought panic. What would I do if a tornado headed my way? Where would I go? My apartment had never felt so flimsy and fragile. On the third floor with most of one wall made of the sliding glass door, my apartment seemed the worst place in the world to be. But where else could I go? I had no car and no way of getting anywhere else. The entire city was blacked out and at a standstill.

I suspected the only people out on the streets tonight would be dangerous to encounter. So, where could I go? What could I do? I'd asked my neighbors what they were planning to do, but nobody had a good answer. Some claimed huddling inside the bathtub would be safest. Others headed for the lowest floors, staying in friends' apartments. One planned to slide under the bed. Another built a cocoon of mattresses and blankets for protection.

I recalled news footage seen over the years of tornado damage. There weren't many safe places to go, as best I could remember. I'd seen footage of flattened houses, cars tossed into trees, and whole blocks of buildings gone. People could survive incredibly powerful tornadoes by rushing to storm shelters underground, but I didn't have one. No storm shelter. No basement. No safe place at all.

While listening to sirens scream all across the city, I dove for my large, walk-in closet, pressed myself against an inside wall and prayed with all my strength. Curled up tight, knees against my chest, head down, I listened intently, remembering people say a tornado sounded like a freight train bearing down on you or like a helicopter landing on your roof.

Curled up in that closet during one of the worst nights of my life, I waited, listened, and prayed. Every now and then, I crept out to peer through my window at the menacing sky or slipped outside my apartment to check again with neighbors to see if they'd heard anything new. I kept my radio close and carried my flashlight with me.

In that endless 24 hours on April 3 and 4, 1974, more than 100 tornadoes tore across 13 states, leaving a path of death and destruction behind. None of us would ever forget this night, filled with fear and tension. We never knew where a twister would strike next or if we'd come through safely amid the sirens, warnings, and dreadful news reports. It was a nightmare for everyone who survived.

Through it all there was no truly safe place, no refuge, except in God, and while I prayed that night, I felt his presence watching over us all.

*W*hy are you downcast,
O my soul?
Why so disturbed within me?
Put your hope in God,
for I will yet praise him,
my Savior and my God.

—PSALM 42:11 NIV

A Safe Place

*So many terrors and troubles confront us,
so many dangers and calamities. Is anyone ever
completely safe? Only when we trust God,
do we know peace and assurance in
the shelter of his care.*

Sometimes our faith delivers us
from difficulties, and sometimes
it delivers us in difficulties.
Either way, God honors our faith
and He gets the glory...
I'm inclined to believe that God
can get greater glory at times
by giving grace to live with
our suffering than power
to escape it.

—WARREN W. WIERSBE, *WHY US? WHEN BAD
THINGS HAPPEN TO GOD'S PEOPLE*

Remember the wonders he
has done.

—PSALM 105:5 NIV

*Disasters strike. No time to prepare. Help us,
Lord, stay close to you. Deepen our trust
and faith in you.*
Amen.

*For thou hast been a strength to
the poor, a strength to the needy
in his distress, a refuge from
the storm.*

—Isaiah 25:4 KJV

Everything's Gone

*She picks at the bits and pieces of her life
amid sodden, fire-scorched debris.
She looks up and says, "Everything's gone."
Then she smiles in her sorrow, and says,
"But look at how much others care,
thank God."*

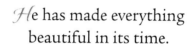

*H*e has made everything
beautiful in its time.

—ECCLESIASTES 3:11 NIV

What Matters Most

*No matter how broken my life, God can create
something new from the pieces, like a quilt
made of scraps, leftovers of a better time but
warming nonetheless.*

Amazing Gains

Just when all seems hopeless, prayer lifts us like
a wave on the ocean. A sturdy craft, prayer
doesn't hide from pain, but uses it like the force
of the sea to move us to a new place of insight,
patience, courage, and sympathy. Always, it is
God's hand beneath the surface holding us up.

The steadfast love of the Lord
never ceases,
his mercies never come to
an end;
they are new every morning;
great is your faithfulness.
"The Lord is my portion," says
my soul,
"therefore I will hope in him."

LAMENTATIONS 3:22–24 NRSV

To all survivors I have one bit of encouragement, for I know after every disaster there is an aftermath. Long after the headlines are history, the hurt and healing continue. The few others who have known similar circumstances can understand. Let them help. . . . And most of all God offers strength beyond all possible comprehension. The One who saved me from the tragedy of my life and brought me through the aftermath makes me supremely grateful that I am alive.

—SANDY PURL, *AM I ALIVE?*

Thank you, Lord, for reaching out and
drawing me under your wings. Even though I
am just one of billions of people who need you,
your love is so great that you know my troubles,
are concerned for my welfare, and are working
to renew my dreams. I am so blessed to have
you to turn to when I am faced with a calamity,
and I am so very grateful that I have you to
lean on. I praise you with all my heart.
Amen.

Faith or Fear

*Beneath our feet the earth trembles. No solid
ground beneath us. Will our hearts tremble,
too? Or will we walk with faith?*

At disappointment and losses
which are the effect of
Providential acts, I never repine;
because I am sure the allwise
Disposer of events knows better
than we do what is best for us, or
what we deserve.

—GEORGE WASHINGTON

God is our refuge and strength,
an ever-present help
in trouble.

—PSALM 46:1 NIV

The Right Place to Be

After the storm, they cautiously push open their closet door and creep from their hiding place. How bad is it? They see destruction everywhere. Nothing left untouched, except for one safe spot—the closet in which the whole family crouched, pressed tight together, frightened, holding one another, praying. One thing remains, upright and safe—their hiding place in time of trouble, their sanctuary, the right place to be.

Nothing Can Separate Us

When disaster shatters our lives, God is our rock, and nothing can separate us from him. Indeed, nothing can separate us from his love.

Be strong and courageous; do
not be frightened or dismayed,
for the Lord your God is with
you wherever you go.

—JOSHUA 1:9 NRSV

*I cannot wander so far
in any direction,
vigilant God, that you are
not already there.*

You're
Not Alone

*D*raw near to God, and he will
draw near to you.

—JAMES 4:8 NRSV

When God Seems Far Away

A long with life's blessings, there are struggles, pain, and loss. While we never welcome these things, we all must go through them. At such times we most keenly feel our need for intervention, and we call out to God.

But what if no answer comes and it seems as if God himself has forgotten us? What if our faith in him is shaken to its very core, and still he is silent? Interestingly, the Bible is full of such themes: men and women of faith crying out to God from their deeply troubled souls. Even Jesus, while he died, called out to his Father, asking why he had forsaken him. Yet, in those times when it seems God is far away, in reality, he is holding us close to his heart.

*G*od was there each step of the
way. When we encountered the
biggest obstacles and
experienced the greatest
discouragement, I felt his
presence most.

—Daphne Gray, *Yes, You Can, Heather!*

Light in Darkness

*N*o darkness is black enough to hide you, Lord,
for there is always light even if I sometimes
misplace it. Just when I'm ready to give up,
there it shines through caregivers, family,
friends; through my renewed energy to choose
treatments and recovery. I'm absolutely certain
you are the sender of this light.

Lord, you have seen each time when I've been abandoned by those in whose love I have trusted. You have known the loneliness in my soul. I must confess to you that it causes me to wonder if your love has failed me, too. I need you to assure me that you are still here and that you will always stay with me.

In my distress I cried unto the
Lord, and he heard me.

—Psalm 120:1 KJV

Help!

I prayed but got no answer,
I believed but nothing changed,
I waited and grew anxious,
God, help my failing faith!

*Lord, I am weary and cannot find my way.
The nights seem endless and thick with
a fog that engulfs my spirit, but I have faith in
you, my Lord and my light. Faith that you
will help me take another step when I feel I can
no longer walk on my own. Faith that
you will be the beacon of hope that guides my
way through the darkness. Faith that this, too,
shall pass and that I will know joy again.
Amen.*

Rest in Me

*When the nights seem long, the days feel like a
struggle, and the spirit is weary,
we find a resting place in God's enduring love,
and we know that his plan for us is good.
This is the true meaning of letting go and letting
God's higher will be done in our lives.*

*D*o not let your hearts be
troubled. Believe in God, believe
also in me. In my Father's house
there are many dwelling places. If
it were not so, would I have told
you that I go to prepare a place
for you? And if I go and prepare
a place for you, I will come again
and will take you to myself, so
that where I am, there you
may be also.

—John 14:1–4 NRSV

God's Heartbeat

*In the silence of despair, we hear nothing
but the lonely beating of our own heart.
In the silence of faith, however, rhythms of the
world around us remind us that God's heart
beats nearby.*

How long, O Lord? Will you
forget me forever?
How long will you hide your face
from me?
How long must I bear pain
in my soul,
and have sorrow in my heart
all day long?
How long shall my enemy
be exalted over me?

—PSALM 13:1-2 NRSV

When we walk along a clear
road feeling fine, and someone
takes our arm to help us, as
likely as not we shall impatiently
shake him off; but when we are
caught in a rough country in the
dark, with a storm getting up
and our strength spent,
and someone takes our arm to
help us, we shall thankfully
lean on him. And God wants us
to feel that our way through
life is rough and perplexing,
so that we may learn thankfully
to lean on him.

—J. I. PACKER, *KNOWING GOD*

O Lord, you alone are my hope.

—PSALM 71:5 NLT

When the Darkness Won't Lift

*D*epression: It's a word we use casually, lightly ignoring the fact that true depression—whether its cause is biological or brought about by life events—can be utterly devastating. The depressed person is emotionally paralyzed, cut off from the stream of daily life. And the condition is self-perpetuating: Just finding the energy to seek help can seem like an insurmountable task.

So how do people find their way out of the darkness and into the light? The motivations to seek help and the ways people find to lift themselves out of the pit of depression are as varied as individual personalities. And God is always there, quietly encouraging us to seek the light.

I would rather walk with God
in the dark than go alone
in the light.

—MARY GARDINER BRAINARD

Understanding in Action

*The best listeners are often silent, the depth of
their understanding revealed by their actions.
God is one such listener.*

There is no darkness so great
that Jesus cannot dispel it.

—CORRIE TEN BOOM, *A PRISONER AND YET...*

God, Have You Left Me Alone?

Anthony's life wasn't perfect, but then, whose is? Actually, despite some rough edges, things were going quite well. His small-scale clothing business was steadily growing, he had just purchased a nice home, he was married to a wonderful woman, and the future looked promising.

With his life moving in a generally positive direction, Anthony just wasn't prepared for what happened next. Not realizing that the many hours he was having to invest in keeping his business running was causing his wife to be disenchanted with their relationship, Anthony was devastated when she told him she wanted a divorce. Try as he might to persuade her to stay and work on their problems, she had made up her mind. With his marriage suddenly and unexpectedly over, Anthony plummeted into despair, and the loneliness he felt was simply unbearable.

Anthony hadn't been a person who prayed a lot, but he did believe in God, and he tried to ease his loneliness by talking with God. His prayers, however, seemed to reach no higher than the ceiling of his now-empty home. He kept asking if God had left him alone, too? He felt abandoned, and he believed he had no one if God wasn't there.

The clothing business—the thing that had been instrumental in destroying his marriage—now became Anthony's saving grace. It was the one thing that kept him going through the motions of life when he felt as if he would rather just lock himself away and hide. And it was through the business that he met Marge and Joan—two seamstresses with whom he contracted to repair some of the "seconds" he had purchased to sell in his store.

Early in the week, Anthony would drop off boxes of clothing at the women's shop, and they would invite him to stay for a cup of tea. Anthony found himself enjoying their company, and his aching soul received a bit of comfort as new friendships emerged.

To his delight, Anthony discovered that he and Marge shared a common interest: Both

played keyboards in a band. The two would talk about music styles, musicians, and songs they knew and loved. Marge would loan Anthony CDs of popular contemporary inspirational artists, and Anthony found that their music uplifted his heart and mind.

Meanwhile, a place of worship that Joan attended had a band that was looking for a keyboard player. She mentioned the position to Anthony, and he looked into it, showed up for some rehearsals, and ended up being just the person for the job.

Today, Anthony is convinced that it was no mistake that his need for meaningful relationships in his life led him to Joan and Marge. For it was through these two women that Anthony has become connected with a caring church community. Relationships he has built there have helped fill the vacancy in his heart, and through community with people of faith, Anthony has rediscovered the faith of his youth—a vibrant, relevant relationship with God.

"I had never been so alone in my life as when my wife left me," Anthony said, "but I've also never been more fulfilled in my relationships as I am now that God has become the key player in my life. I only wish I had known earlier how much his presence makes a difference in the relationships I have with other people. But while I can't change what's past, this I am sure of: God will never abandon me, and he can bring healing to a lonely heart."

Pain Is Better Shared

To be alone and in pain is so much worse than being surrounded by friends and family who care.

Someone is there, I realized.
Someone is watching life as it
unfolds on this planet. More,
Someone is there who loves me.
It was a startling feeling of wild
hope, a feeling so new and
overwhelming that it seemed
fully worth risking my life on.

—PHILIP YANCEY, *DISAPPOINTMENT WITH GOD*

It is you who light my lamp;
the Lord, my God, lights
up my darkness.
This God—his way is perfect;
the promise of the Lord
proves true;
he is a shield for all who take
refuge in him.

—PSALM 18:28, 30 NRSV

*O*ur hope is built on our Lord's faithfulness. He's there with you now. Trust Him. And then expectantly anticipate that at the right time and in the way that's most creative to you and all concerned, He will intervene and infuse you with exactly what you need. What an exciting way to live!

—LLOYD JOHN OGILVIE, *GOD'S BEST FOR MY LIFE*

The Loneliest Number

*T*he words "alone," "lonely," and "abandoned" all contain the word "one." When we believe we stand by ourselves to face life's difficulties—just one person against the world—we will often feel alone, lonely, and abandoned. But in the words "community," "fellowship," and "family," there is no longer the possibility that one might be left to stand alone.

Because the Lord is my Shepherd, I have everything I need! He lets me rest in the meadow grass and leads me beside the quiet streams. He gives me new strength. He helps me do what honors him the most. Even when walking through the dark valley of death I will not be afraid, for you are close beside me, guarding, guiding all the way.

—PSALM 23:1–4 TLB

*O*urs is not a cosmic God who is
powerful and holy, but
indifferent. He knows when we
hurt, where we are weak, and
how we are tempted. Jesus is not
only our Savior, but our loving
Lord who sympathizes with us.
Rejoice in the greatness of His
love for us.

—JOHN F. MACARTHUR, JR., *DRAWING NEAR*

*Reach out to me, a child again, lost, frightened,
and alone with few answers for comfort. Stay
with me until I fall asleep and be here if I awake
scared. Let me be a child tonight, Lord.
Tomorrow I'll be big and strong and all grown
up, but for now, find me, hold me.*

If loneliness is your problem, make it a priority in your Christian service to start solving loneliness for somebody else. . . . Put yourself out for this person, not in an ostentatious way that makes him feel embarrassed and patronized, but in a sincere desire to form a good relationship.

In such an atmosphere of self-giving love, loneliness—crippling, corrosive loneliness—simply cannot survive.

—JOHN HAGGAI, WIN OVER LONELINESS

Sharing the Burden

So much of the crippling weight we carry upon our shoulders can be alleviated by simply understanding that we don't have to carry the burden alone. God is always there, walking beside us, and ready to take the entire load from us should we only ask him to.

Psalm 121

I lift up my eyes to the hills—
from where will my help come?
My help comes from the Lord,
who made heaven and earth. He
will not let your foot be moved;
he who keeps you
will not slumber.
He who keeps Israel
will neither slumber nor sleep.
The Lord is your keeper;
the Lord is your shade at
your right hand.
The sun shall not strike you by
day, nor moon by night.
The Lord will keep you
from all evil;
he will keep your life.
The Lord will keep your going
out and your coming in
from this time on and
forevermore.

*B*e encouraged, child of God. He loves you even in the midst of your pain. He loves you even when you don't love Him. He loves you when you feel utterly alone. He loves you with an everlasting love. Your suffering can take many things away from you—your health, your happiness, your prosperity, your popularity, your friends, your career, even your family. But there's one thing suffering can't take away; it can't take away the love of God.

—RAY PRITCHARD, *THE ROAD BEST TRAVELED*

Seeking Your Angels

*W*e're seldom, if ever, truly "in this alone." In the midst of trouble, we may feel dreadfully isolated, but healing rarely comes without a little or a lot of help from outside, from those people in our lives who act as our earthly guardian angels extending God's help and love.

Seeking your personal angels might literally mean going out and looking for the right person to help with your particular problem. Just as often, though, it means learning to recognize the angels already knocking at your door. Pain and sorrow can blind us to the compassionate friends nearby who are eager and able to help us on the road to recovery. If you're ready to seek healing, take a good look around. Your earthly angel might be standing right in front of you.

*G*reat faith is not the faith that
walks always in the light and
knows no darkness, but the faith
that perseveres in spite of God's
seeming silences, and that faith
will most certainly and surely get
its reward.

—FATHER ANDREW SDC

Truth or Circumstances?

*N*o one knows the mind of God, nor why
he chooses to work the way he does.
But in our most difficult circumstances,
we will miss the peace of his presence unless
we persevere in trusting that he is always
faithful and always good.

Dear God, waiting for you is the hardest part of life. Not knowing. Not understanding. Not being able to figure things out. And when you don't provide answers right away, I feel as if I'll go crazy. But when I stop a moment and think about it, it makes sense that there will be times when you ask me to just trust you, when you'll challenge my rhetoric about believing in you and teach me to be patient. So here I am. I'll be still and wait for you.

Filling the Void With God

Traumatic events leave a void in our souls that only a closer relationship with God can fill. By asking God to help us through hard times, we truly come to understand that we are never alone and that sadness is only a precursor to joy and pain a precursor to healing.

Difference, Not Indifference

Just because God's way of helping us is different than we hoped or expected, it doesn't mean he is indifferent to our cries for help. We must believe that he knows what is truly best for us and is actively doing what is best for us.

*L*ove the Lord with all
your might;
Turn to him, seek him day
and night…

—WILLIAM WORDSWORTH, "PETER BELL"

How lonely we are when trouble strikes. Send
us a sign, Lord. We long for a message, a hand
reaching toward us. And just as God promised,
we're visited by a Presence in dream and
daylight revelations, and we are grateful for
God's personal, one-on-one caring.

*T*he Lord is near to all who call
on him, to all who call on him in
truth. He fulfills the desire of all
who fear him; he also hears their
cry, and saves them. The Lord
watches over all who love him.

—PSALM 145:18–20

I Will Not Leave You Comfortless

In our worst moments, shattered by pain in body, mind, and spirit, God has promised not to leave us alone or without comfort.

Right now, wherever you are, you can turn around and He'll be there welcoming you. Waiting to prove His love to you.

—ETHEL WATERS, *TO ME IT'S WONDERFUL*

*Do not be grieved, for the joy
of the Lord is your strength.*

—Nehemiah 8:10 NRSV

Heavenly Comfort

Life, once filled with sunlight and promise, has
been colored by loss and is now all storm and
shadow. Use my tears, Lord, as the showers
needed to bring rainbows. Shine your love on
me as the sun; lift my eyes so I can see even the
smallest curves of hope in the dark sky.

Getting Through

When a long-term relationship comes to an
end, it's natural to mourn the loss of a
companion and to grieve the death of a
particular way of life. But we can mourn and
grieve only for so long, then we must ask God
to give us the grace and the courage to
finally close that door and walk toward a new
door waiting to be opened. We must take the
next step God has for us.

When the anguish of loss
   overwhelms us,
and we feel there's no reason
   to live.
We must look deep within to
   find meaning
and to know we've still so much
   to give.

I sit in what once was and grieve what is lost forever. And yet words once heard float like mind-perfume, opening up a floodgate of memory, recalling the moments when those words were spoken. And I am comforted. Thank you, O God, for the gift of remembering.

Consoling Love

Our loss touches God's heart deeply. He created the one for whom we grieve, and he knows very well the irreplaceable nature of the relationship we shared. God does not minimize or misunderstand our pain. He weeps with us and longs to console us with his love.

*W*eeping may linger for
the night,
but joy comes with the morning.

—PSALM 30:5 NRSV

My grief feels as if it will never subside, God. Everything within me melts like wax when I wake up in the morning and realize all over again what has happened. My life is forever changed. Sometimes I wonder if you are there, but I know you have promised always to be with me. Please hold me close.
Amen.

As you face death with all its impact on your feelings and your way of life, the greatest force for sustaining you and bringing meaning to the apparently meaningless is your ability to see life not with physical preoccupations but in the light of the New Testament revelation.

—EDGAR N. JACKSON, *WHEN SOMEONE DIES*

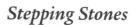

Stepping Stones

*Life's tragedies make us into stepping stones.
Without suffering, we would be like lumps of
clay that have not yet been fired in the potter's
oven to a transforming state of usefulness.*

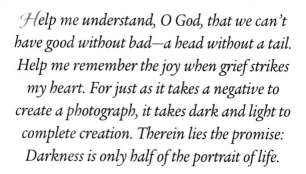

*Help me understand, O God, that we can't
have good without bad—a head without a tail.
Help me remember the joy when grief strikes
my heart. For just as it takes a negative to
create a photograph, it takes dark and light to
complete creation. Therein lies the promise:
Darkness is only half of the portrait of life.*

*U*se the gift of
listening.... Listening is hard.
The sound of our own voices
may be therapy for us, but it is
not necessarily healing for the
wounded griever. During a time
of shock people need to repeat
their story over and over again.
You may think they would grow
weary of giving details,
or telling what happened, but
that isn't the case at all.

—BILLY GRAHAM,
FACING DEATH AND THE LIFE AFTER

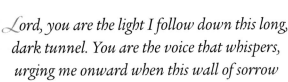

Get Up, Get Over, Get On

When the despair that comes with the pain of a
loss immobilizes us and makes us feel powerless,
God gives us the inner fortitude and grace we
need to get up, get over the suffering,
and get on with our lives.

Lord, you are the light I follow down this long,
dark tunnel. You are the voice that whispers,
urging me onward when this wall of sorrow
seems insurmountable. You are the hand
that reaches out and grabs mine when I feel
as if I'm sinking in despair. You alone, Lord,
are the waters that fill me when I am dried
of all hope and faith. I thank you, Lord,
for although I may feel like giving up,
you have not given up on me.
Amen.

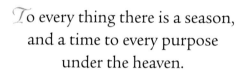

To every thing there is a season,
and a time to every purpose
under the heaven.

—ECCLESIASTES 3:1 KJV

When we are helpless and
without relief or are devoid of
comfort, God is most willing to
aid and comfort us.

—E. M. BOUNDS, *OBTAINING ANSWERS TO PRAYER*

When Loss Saddens Your Life

*Is there anything more painful than the death
of a loved one—a precious parent, spouse,
friend, child? When such a loss occurs,
we feel the world should stop turning; all life
should freeze in its tracks, just as time seems to
have stopped for us. And yet, life goes on,
despite our protests. And, impossible though it
seems at first, healing can and does take place.
With honest grieving, understanding friends,
and the passage of time, it becomes possible to
cope and begin living for ourselves again.
After all, it does not dishonor the dead to take
care of the living, even as we treasure our
memories of our lost ones.*

Help me grieve and go on ... go on in new ways you will reveal to me, Lord, as I make my faltering way as far as I can. Hold me while I name and mourn all I have lost, weeping and wailing like the abandoned child I feel I am. Then, in time and with you to lean on, I can focus on what I have left.

Beyond Sorrow

When the loss of someone we dearly love brings a cold darkness to our lives, it seems that darkness will be forever with us and our hearts will never feel joy again. We believe then that night will never end and day will never come. Yet the darkness will leave and the night will end when we hold on to our Lord, for he will bring light back into our lives. And in that light, our hopes will be renewed and a joy will reside in our hearts once again.

Life is real! Life is earnest!
And the grave is not its goal;
Dust thou art, to dust returnest;
Was not spoken of the soul.

—HENRY WADSWORTH LONGFELLOW,
"A PSALM OF LIFE"

*Grief, O God of current and tides, is taking me
somewhere new. Feeling your guiding hand,
I will hold on and keep moving.*

Healing Waters

*In my hour of need, I turn my eyes inward to a
place where God's strength flows like a river of
healing waters. I immerse myself in the current,
and I am renewed.*

*E*very good thing that comes into our lives carries within it the power to make us fear its loss. Yet, at those distressing times when we lose our grip on the things we think will save us, there is something beyond the fear. It is the recognition that loss can carry hope along with it: the hope that what is taken away will be replaced by something even better.

—JOSEPH BIUSO AND BRIAN NEWMAN,
RECEIVING LOVE

*F*or the believer, death is a transition, not a termination.

—LESLIE B. FLYNN, *THE SUSTAINING POWER OF HOPE*

A Brighter Tomorrow

For just as the harshest winter always gives
way to the warm blush of spring, the season of
our suffering will give way to a brighter
tomorrow, where change becomes a catalyst
for new growth and spiritual maturity,
and we are able to move on with the
joyfulness of being alive.

Dear God, help me understand that what may
appear to be a "good-bye" is really only an
"until we meet again."
Amen.

Miracles Come in Twos

Jennie thought this had to be the best day of her life. Not only had she and her husband, Rich, just learned that she was pregnant but that twins were on the way. Because they had been trying to conceive for years and had run into countless health-related obstacles, they thought it would never happen, but the proof was in the ultrasound image they took home from the doctor's office.

Four months into the pregnancy, Jennie had to be rushed to the emergency room late one night. The doctor on duty attended to Jennie with a calm and professional precision, making her as comfortable as possible before quietly telling her that she was in an extremely delicate situation. Jennie panicked, grabbing Rich's hand for support while the doctor continued to examine her. When the doctor put the stethoscope on Jennie's stomach, the look on her face was tight and unreadable, but Jennie could sense that something was terribly wrong. Her intuition was confirmed when additional tests showed the fetuses had died in the womb.

For over a month, Rich did what he could to comfort Jennie, but she was inconsolable. She had given the twins names and continued to speak into her tummy as if they were still alive. She simply could not—would not—accept that she would not have children.

As the strain of Jennie's grief and his own sadness took its toll on Rich, he realized he would have to be the stronger one at this dark time. He knew that if he could not help Jennie cope, she might never recover from her mourning. Lying in bed at night, he prayed for direction as he watched his wife toss and turn from a sedative-induced sleep. He prayed that the right answer would soon come and that his wife would be able to move through her suffering and accept the loss of their twins.

As the days went on, no big miracles occurred, but Rich could definitely see that Jennie was getting stronger. She used the sleeping sedatives less, she started eating better, and she even began to do one of her favorite hobbies before the loss—jigsaw puzzles. It calmed her, and Rich was thrilled when she came to him one day and put her arms around him. It was the first sign of affection he had felt from her in a long time.

Jennie finally came to accept the loss of the twins and even of any possibility of giving birth. Her doctor confirmed she would never be able to bring a child to full term. Yet what proved to Rich that God's grace was indeed flowing in their lives was the morning Jennie asked him to sit down and discuss the possibility of adoption. The glow in her eyes when she talked about loving and caring for a child that no one else wanted assured Rich that everything was going to be all right. When they eventually went into the adoption agency for an interview, the woman who assisted them told them they would have no trouble at all, as they were a loving and stable couple.

Four months later, Jennie and Rich brought home not one, but two, beautiful baby girls whose mother and father had been killed in a plane crash. They were given the very same names that Jennie had once hoped to give her own twins, Hope and Faith, and they were loved just as much as if they had indeed been born from Jennie's womb. As Rich watched Jennie mother and fuss over their new girls, he knew in his heart that God not only had heard his prayers but also had provided them with a miracle.

Make that two miracles!

It's lonely, Lord, being left. The burden to carry on alone bends me over like a willow in the wind. And yet, I feel you coming close to me. Thank you, Lord.

The Mystery of the Eternal

The passing of a dear one often leaves us wondering "Why, God, why?" If we knew that death is the beginning of a new mystery, a new adventure to unfold, we would feel joy for those who leave this earth and joy for those yet to leave.

*S*ee, the home of God is among mortals.
He will dwell with them;
they will be his peoples,
and God himself will be with them;
he will wipe every tear from their eyes.
Death will be no more;
mourning and crying and pain will be no more,
for the first things have passed away.

—REVELATION 21:3–4 NRSV

In times of loss and sorrow,
when hearts are dark with pain,
we find a source of light within
to make life bright again.

*G*od of my heart, bring me comfort and peace
in this time of confusion and sorrow. Help me
know that, although things are bleak, there is
always a brighter tomorrow.

*I*t's one thing to write about God's promises; it's quite another to remember those promises when you need them! Grief? Yes, she would sorrow a long time over the loss of her friend. But even as she mourned she would enjoy the sure knowledge that separation is temporary.

—SANDRA DENGLER,
FANNY CROSBY—WRITER OF 8000 SONGS

I Cry Out

In the depth of my pain, I cry out to God. In grief and sorrow, in loss and anguish, I cry out to God. When I am overwhelmed and cannot bear another moment, I cry out to God. And he hears my cry. He listens and cares and answers, as he always has throughout all time.

You will search in vain for some "reason" that makes the death of your beloved seem fair, just, and understandable. However, God works after the fact of the death to bring meaning to your life.

—WAYNE E. OATES, *YOUR PARTICULAR GRIEF*

*T*herefore we do not lose heart.
Though outwardly we are
wasting away, yet inwardly we are
being renewed day by day. For
our light and momentary
troubles are achieving for us
an eternal glory that far
outweighs them all. So we fix our
eyes not on what is seen,
but on what is unseen. For what
is seen is temporary, but what is
unseen is eternal.

—2 CORINTHIANS 4:16-18

*B*lessed are those who trust in
the Lord.

—JEREMIAH 17:7 NRSV

His Whispering Voice

This is our darkest hour when we feel we cannot suffer any worse. Yet, something inside whispers to us, "For everything there is a season," and we notice the faint glimmer of hope at the end of this long, dark tunnel of despair. The more we focus on the voice, the louder it becomes. The more we seek the light, the brighter it becomes. This is God's love and compassion for us making itself known, and in his growing presence, we become stronger and our faith is renewed.

Connect With God

When we lose a spouse, we must take time to go within and reaffirm our connection with God. Once we are able to feel God's presence at work in our lives, we will know that we already have all we need to help us move beyond the grief and begin to live and love again.

*P*raise be to the God and Father
of our Lord Jesus Christ,
the Father of compassion and
the God of all comfort,
who comforts us in all our
troubles, so that we can comfort
those in any trouble with the
comfort we ourselves have
received from God.

—2 CORINTHIANS 1:3-4 NIV

*Lord, the familiar is disappearing from
neighborhood and nature, and we grieve
the loss. Yet, we're resurrection people, unafraid
of endings because of the promise of beginnings.
On the other hand, we must learn restraint:
Help us, God, to temper our actions
with wisdom.
Amen.*

Moving On

The pain of losing someone dear to us or watching a relationship come to an end can be overwhelming. We feel bereft and alone, confused and lost, certain that we will hurt like this forever. But with God's strength, we can move on.

*D*ark days do not last forever. The clouds are always moving, though very slowly. The person in the midst of depression is certain, of course, that the clouds are not moving.... One of the most helpful things we can do for a friend at such a time is to stand by that friend in quiet confidence, and assure him or her that this, too, shall pass.

—GRANGER E. WESTBERG, *GOOD GRIEF*

*D*o not be afraid, little flock, for it is your Father's good pleasure to give you the kingdom.

—LUKE 12:32 NRSV

Like a toddler who falls more than he stands,
I'm pulling myself upright in the aftermath of
death. I know you as a companion, God of
mending hearts, and feel you steadying me.
Thank you for the gift of resilience. Lead me to
others who have hurt and gone on;
I need to see how it's done.

Eternally Yours

If you have suffered the loss of someone you
love, remember that, although his or her body
has gone from this earth, the love you shared
remains an eternal and joyful presence in your
life. Indeed, they will be eternally yours.

Blessed are those who mourn,
for they will be comforted.

—MATTHEW 5:4 NRSV

...in all human sorrows nothing
gives comfort but love and faith.

—LEO TOLSTOY, *ANNA KARENINA*

*We praise you, Lord, for eternal life. And we
thank you for your love for each one of us.
Amen.*